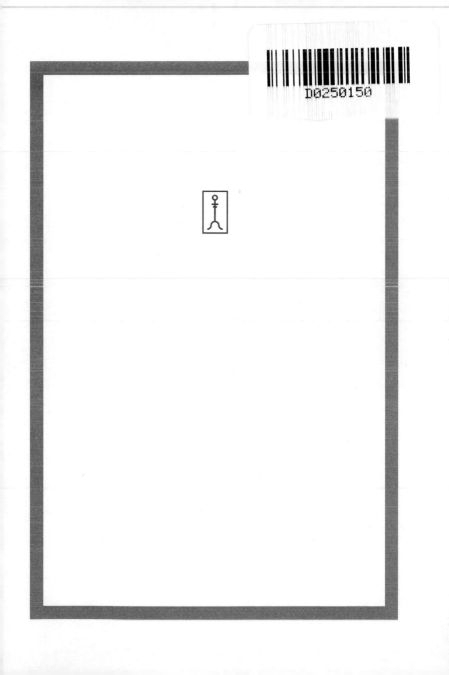

MORE
GEORGE
W
Bushisms

**More of *Slate*'s Accidental Wit and Wisdom
of Our Forty-third President**

EDITED BY JACOB WEISBERG
with a Foreword by Garry Trudeau

FIRESIDE

New York   London   Toronto   Sydney   Singapore

FIRESIDE
Rockefeller Center
1230 Avenue of the Americas
New York, NY 10020

FIRESIDE and colophon are registered
trademarks of Simon & Schuster, Inc.

For information about special discounts for bulk purchases,
please contact Simon & Schuster Special Sales at
1-800-465-6798 or business@simonandschuster.com

Designed by Bonni Leon-Berman
Manufactured in the United States of America
7   9   10   8   6

Library of Congress Cataloging-in-Publication Data
ISBN 0–7432–2519–8
Photo credits appear on page 88.

FOREWORD BY GARRY TRUDEAU

While a great deal of thought and care has gone into the creation of this little volume, it is altogether fitting that none of it was by its author. That credit falls to the book's editor, Jacob Weisberg, whose unmatched bona fides as a curator of Bush family utterances extend back more than a decade. Weisberg cut his fangs on Bush *pere,* whose malapropisms he tracked as a lowly editorial assistant on 1992's *Bushisms: President George Herbert Walker Bush, In His Own Words.* That collection quickly died in the bookstores, but since it was published shortly before Bush senior tanked in the general election, Weisberg—correctly, in my judgment—was not held directly responsible. Thus, when George W. Bush suddenly emerged a few years later, making even less sense than his father, Weisberg was uniquely positioned, like an Arabic-speaking CIA agent on September 12. He immediately volunteered his services to Michael Kinsley, his editor at *Slate,* offering to set up a kind of conservatory for second wave Bushisms. Kinsley, famously supportive of folk art generally and outsider prose in particular, quickly signed off on the archival feature from which this collection—and its bestselling predecessor—is drawn.

Weisberg is the first to admit that, in cataloging and documenting Bushisms, he has had many enablers. Since his other duties at *Slate* precluded his being everywhere the president appeared in public, he has counted heavily on a posse of like-minded aficionados—editors, reporters, and amateur collectors—to send in Bushisms from the field not for recognition or monetary gain but out of love for the idiom. For this reason, this book is essentially a connoisseur's collection, created, as many Web-based projects are, out of the shared affection and labor of a few devoted souls—in this case, the tightly knit Bushism community.

Their work has not always been easy. The White House now scrubs presidential transcripts clean of the more delightful gaffes, and members of self-selecting, partisan audiences cannot be relied on to faithfully report utterances that might alarm the rest of the country. Even if they were so inclined, like eyewitnesses at accidents, they would be unlikely to agree on exactly what happened the moment the president's train of thought flew off the rails. Some things Bush says simply defy reconstruction.

Of course, the president is now more disciplined, winging it far less, staying on TelePrompTer and thus mostly out of trouble. And yet there are moments when Bush cannot help being himself, when he feels so overcome with exuberance, so in "wings-take-dreams" mode, that he will tear his eyes from his text and say things like: "We'll be a country where the fabrics are made up of group and loving centers." Or: "The way I like to put it is this. There's no bigger issue for the president to remind the moms and dads of America, if you happen to have a child, be fortunate to have a child."

That Bush risks going off-book at all is not because he forgets about his peculiar verbal disability. It's because it never occurs to him that it might be important for the Leader of the Free World to express himself with clarity and coherence. Just as the mark of the educated man is a humbling awareness of how little he knows (thus the signature insecurity of professors), the most salient feature of the unschooled is cluelessness, the inability to grasp one's own condition. Bush is plenty smart—and he's technically educated—but because of his natural incuriosity about the wider world, Bush has fought a crippling, life-long battle with ignorance. That he so frequently tells the public he "understands" such-and-such a problem has nothing to do with empathy—it's about reassurance. Don't worry, he seems to say, I really am on top of things; I only talk this way because I'm real.

Or to quote him directly: "I admit it, I am not one of the great linguists."

Enjoy.

INTRODUCTION:
THE YEAR IN BUSHISMS

The predecessor to this volume was published in January 2001, during the brief interval between coronation and inauguration. The book began to sell, George W. Bush was sworn in, and I continued to wonder about one question: How did Bush feel about Bushisms? Was he chuckling along, Reagan-style, or percolating with Nixonian rage?

My puzzlement came to an end a few months later at the White House Correspondents Dinner when the president fulfilled my authorial fantasy by waving *Slate*'s book of *George W. Bushisms* at 1,500 reporters. "Most of you probably didn't know that I have a new book out," he exclaimed, before launching into a reading. Repeating his line, "I believe the human being and fish can coexist peacefully," the president declared: "Anyone can give you a coherent sentence, but something like this takes you into an entirely new dimension." Bush recited several other classics ("make the pie higher," "more and more of our imports come from overseas"), before commending himself again. "Now, ladies and gentlemen, you have to admit, in my sentences I go where no man has gone before," he said.

The performance was, as the president likes to say, fabulous! Bill Clinton used to show up at these events and self-deprecate through clenched teeth. But Bush wasn't just rolling with the punches, he was running with them. If our president was an international laughingstock, he was at least a laughing laughingstock. Of course, W. being W., he committed a Bushism or two while discussing Bushisms. "I've coined new words, like, 'misunderstanding' and 'Hispanically,'" he noted. I believe he intended to say "misunderestimate," one of his signatures, but believing that to be an actual word, he was temporarily boggled by his own prepared text. So what do you call it when Bush, attempting a Bushism, stumbles and accidentally uses a word *correctly*? A reverse Bushism? A Bushism*ism*?

In any case, it was impossible not to reciprocate this display of presidential goodwill. I soon found myself paroling Bushisms that might be excused as mere quirks of West Texas dialect, such as "nucular" for "nuclear," "tireously" for "tirelessly," "explayed" for "displayed," and, in what sounded like a kind of Tex-Mex omelet, "Infitada," for "Intifada." I let Bush's waving to Stevie Wonder at a concert—a visual Bushism, you had to see it to appreciate it—pass without comment.

When Bush sent the yen plunging by saying he'd spoken with the Japanese prime minister about "devaluation" (he was supposed to say "deflation"), I let it slide. And when he provoked a diplomatic crisis by accusing North Korea of violating agreements on nuclear weapons (there's only one agreement and no evidence of North Korea breaking it), that passed unmentioned as well. Surely, as one White House spinner proposed, the president was referring to *possible future agreements* that North Korea *might* sign and *then* violate. I found you could explain away a lot of slips once you bought into the notion that, as one aide put it, *that's just how the president speaks.*

After September 11, I stopped publishing Bushisms in *Slate.* This decision provoked considerable complaint from readers. Bush had urged the nation to get back to normal. What could be more normal than making fun of W.? Who was I to violate a presidential directive? My feeling, though, was that Bushisms had ceased to be funny. If the commander-in-chief was indeed a few bricks short of a load, we'd all better shut up about it and pray Dick Cheney was ordering the salmon. I figured I'd wait until The Evil One had been finished off, then get back to my collection. But six months on, Osama bin Laden was no longer much discussed, at least in Republican circles. And I had to admit, I was finding the Bushisms that readers and friends continued to send in funny again. So *Slate*'s "Bushism of the Day" feature came back to life.

My job had not gotten any easier during the interim. Under the ever-watchful eyes of Karen Hughes and Karl Rove, the war-president was speaking in public less frequently and less spontaneously. The image team was no longer turning him loose on audiences with five hours sleep and no prepared text. In another blow, the White House Press Office began cleaning up its official transcripts of the president's remarks. I was no longer traveling with the president and depended on the verbatim accuracy of these accounts. If Bush said something about people working hard to put food on their families or removing the federal cuff link, would I even hear about it?

Happily, I still have my sources. Karen has gone home to Texas. And, despite Karl's best efforts, there are still those magical days when the president, without enough sleep or exercise, staggers out onto the White House lawn, searches in vain for a TelePrompTer, squints at the distant horizon, and opens his mouth. *"And so, in my State of the— my State of the Union—or state—my speech to the nation, whatever you want to call it, speech to the nation—I asked Americans to give 4,000 years—4,000 hours over the next— the rest of your life—of service to America. That's what I asked—4,000 hours."* If I miss one of these moments, a helpful colleague in attendance or an alert *Slate* reader tuned in to C-Span generally brings it to my attention.

Back to you, Mr. President.

MORE
GEORGE
W
Bushisms

HOORAY

"I want everybody to hear loud and clear that I'm going to be the president of everybody."

—*Washington, D.C., January 18, 2001*

THE NEW NATIONALISM

"Well, it's an unimaginable honor to be the
president during the Fourth of July of this
country. It means what these words say,
for starters. The great inalienable rights of
our country. We're blessed with such values
in America. And I—it's—I'm a proud man to
be the nation based upon such wonderful
values."

*—Visiting the Jefferson Memorial, Washington, D.C.,
July 2, 2001*

BEYOND BELIEF

"I know what I believe. I will continue to
articulate what I believe and what I
believe—I believe what I believe is right."

—*Rome, Italy, July 22, 2001*

THE BLAME GAME

"Presidents, whether things are good or bad, get the blame. I understand that."

—Washington, D.C., May 11, 2001

NOVELTY ITEM

"I'm not a very good novelist. But it'd make a pretty interesting novel."

—On the Florida postelection battle, Austin, Texas, December 5, 2000

RERUN

"We can come together to heal whatever wounds may exist, whatever residuals there may be."

—*With Congressional leaders on Capitol Hill, Washington, D.C., December 18, 2000*

FORGIVING

**"Let me put it to you this way,
I am not a revengeful person."**

—*Interview with* Time *magazine,
December 25, 2000*

SUCCESS I

"I'm hopeful. I know there is a lot of
ambition in Washington, obviously.
But I hope the ambitious realize that they
are more likely to succeed with success
as opposed to failure."

—Interview with the Associated Press, January 18, 2001

SUCCESS II

"And there's no doubt in my mind, not one
doubt in my mind, that we will fail."

—Washington, D.C., October 4, 2001

MIND FULL?

"I am mindful not only of preserving executive powers for myself, but for predecessors as well."

—*Washington, D.C., January 29, 2001*

LOST IN TRANSLATION

"Oftentimes what I try to say in Washington gets filtered and sometimes my words in Washington don't exactly translate directly to the people."

—*Kalamazoo, Michigan, March 27, 2001*

CABINET I

"I can't tell you how good of folks
they are, not only in terms of the jobs they'll
have, but just in the quality of character."

—Press conference, Austin, Texas, December 17, 2000

CABINET II

"I'm going to work with every Cabinet
member to set a series of goals
for each Cabinet."

*—News conference naming his secretaries of energy, labor,
and transportation, Austin, Texas, January 2, 2001*

JOHN

"If he's—the inference is that somehow he thinks slavery is a—is a noble institution— I would—I would strongly reject that assumption. That John Ashcroft is an open-minded, inclusive person."

—Interview with Tom Brokaw, NBC News, January 15, 2001

LINDA

"She is a member of a labor union at one point."

—Announcing his nomination of Linda Chavez as secretary of labor, Austin, Texas, January 2, 2001

"I would have to ask the questioner.
I haven't had a chance to ask the
questioners the question they've been
questioning. On the other hand, I firmly
believe she'll be a fine secretary of labor.
And I've got confidence in Linda Chavez.
She is a—she'll bring an interesting
perspective to the Labor Department."

—*Austin, Texas, January 8, 2001*

"I do remain confident in Linda.
She'll make a fine labor secretary.
From what I've read in the press accounts,
she's perfectly qualified."

—*Ibid*

MEL

"I also have picked a secretary for Housing and Human Development. Mel Martinez from the state of Florida."

—*Announcing his nominee for the Department of Housing and Urban Development, Austin, Texas, December 20, 2000*

NINO

"She's just trying to make sure Anthony gets a good meal—Antonio."

—Telling Tom Brokaw about Laura Bush inviting Justice Antonin Scalia to dinner at the White House, Dateline NBC, *January 14, 2000*

ALAN

"I talked with a good man right here.
We had a very strong discussion about
my confidence in his abilities."

—*After breakfast with Alan Greenspan, Washington, D.C.,*
December 18, 2000

TEDDY

"I must confess, it did confuse some of the folks at the Crawford, Texas, coffee shop when I was traveling around the country with Theodore Kennedy."

—*Chicago, Illinois, May 13, 2002*

BILL

"I think it's time for the president— to allow the president to finish his term, and let him move on and enjoy life and become an active participant in the American system."

—*Austin, Texas, January 8, 2001*

PRIME MINISTER

"We both use Colgate toothpaste."

*—On his relationship with Tony Blair, Camp David,
Maryland, February 23, 2001*

QUEEN

"She was neat."

—*On meeting Queen Elizabeth II, as quoted in*
The Times *of London, July 18, 2001*

DEFENSIVE

"We want to develop defenses that are capable of defending ourselves and defenses capable of defending others."

—*Washington, D.C., March 29, 2001*

CHANGE

**"I think it's very important for world
leaders to understand that when a
new administration comes in, the new
administration will be running the
foreign policy."**

—Interview with USA Today, January 12, 2001

NO DEAL

**"First, we would not accept a treaty that
would not have been ratified, nor a treaty
that I thought made sense for the country."**

*—On the Kyoto accord in an interview with
The Washington Post, April 24, 2001*

CO-DEPENDENT

"Redefining the role of the United States from enablers to keep the peace to enablers to keep the peace from peacekeepers is going to be an assignment."

—*Interview with* The New York Times, *January 14, 2001*

DIPLOMAT

"You saw the president yesterday. I thought he was very forward-leaning, as they say in diplomatic nuanced circles."

—Referring to his meeting with
Russian president Vladimir Putin, Rome, July 23, 2001

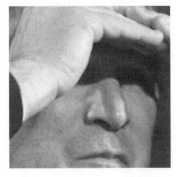

THE OLD WAR

"Russia is no longer our enemy and therefore we shouldn't be locked into a Cold War mentality that says we keep the peace by blowing each other up. In my attitude, that's old, that's tired, that's stale."

—*Des Moines, Iowa, June 8, 2001*

"But I also made it clear to
[Vladimir Putin] that it's important to
think beyond the old days of when we
had the concept that if we blew each
other up, the world would be safe."

—*Washington, D.C., May 1, 2001*

"It's negative to think about blowing
each other up. That's not a positive
thought. That's a Cold War thought.
That's a thought when people were
enemies with each other."

—*Interview with Peggy Noonan,*
The Wall Street Journal, *June 25, 2001*

ENOUGH

"The suicide bombings have increased.
There's too many of them."

—*Albuquerque, New Mexico, August 15, 2001*

LEADER

"After all, a week ago, there were—
Yasser Arafat was boarded up in his building
in Ramallah, a building full of, evidently,
German peace protestors and all kinds of
people. They're now out. He's now free to
show leadership, to lead the world."

—*Washington, D.C., May 2, 2002*

AREA STUDIES

"I understand that the unrest in the Middle East creates unrest throughout the region."

—*Washington, D.C., March 13, 2002*

PESSIMIST

"My administration has been calling upon all the leaders in the—in the Middle East to do everything they can to stop the violence, to tell the different parties involved that peace will never happen."

—*Crawford, Texas, August 13, 2001*

GROUNDED

"These terrorist acts and, you know, the responses have got to end in order for us to get the framework—the groundwork—not framework, the groundwork to discuss a framework for peace, to lay the—all right."

—*Referring to former Senator George Mitchell's report on Middle East peace, Crawford, Texas, August 13, 2001*

EXCEPTION?

"For a century and a half now, America and
Japan have formed one of the great and
enduring alliances of modern times."

—Tokyo, Japan, February 18, 2002

CHANGELING

"The United States and Russia are in the
midst of a transformationed relationship
that will yield peace and progress."

*—White House press conference with Vladimir Putin,
November 13, 2001*

35

SICKNESS

"We spent a lot of time talking about Africa, as we should. Africa is a nation that suffers from incredible disease."

—Gothenburg, Sweden, June 14, 2001

BLACK HUMOR

"Do you have blacks, too?"

—To Brazilian president Fernando Cardoso, as quoted in Der Spiegel, *May 19, 2002*

NO WAY, JOSE

"Neither in French nor in English nor in Mexican."

—*Declining to answer reporters' questions at the Summit of the Americas, Quebec City, Canada, April 21, 2001*

DIPLOMACY THING

"This foreign policy stuff is a little frustrating."

—*As quoted by the* New York Daily News, *April 23, 2002*

MR. UNDERESTIMATE

"The folks who conducted to act on our
country on September 11 made a big
mistake. They underestimated America.
They underestimated our resolve, our
determination, our love for freedom.
They misunderestimated the fact that
we love a neighbor in need.
They misunderestimated the
compassion of our country. I think they
misunderestimated the will and
determination of the commander
in chief, too."

—*At the CIA, Langley, Virginia, September 26, 2001*

ON BALANCE

"But all in all, it's been a fabulous year for Laura and me."

—Showing a new rug in the Oval Office,
December 21, 2001

JERRY'S KIDS

"They didn't think we were a nation
that could conceivably sacrifice for
something greater than our self; that we
were soft, that we were so self-absorbed
and so materialistic that we wouldn't
defend anything we believed in. My, were
they wrong. They just were reading
the wrong magazine, or watching the
wrong Springer show."

—*Washington, D.C., March 12, 2001*

TRADE

"It's very important for folks to understand that when there's more trade, there's more commerce."

—*Quebec City, Canada, April 21, 2001*

UNFORMED

"I'm confident we can work with
Congress to come up with an economic
stimulus package that will send a clear
signal to the risk-takers and capital
formators of our country."

—Washington, D.C., September 17, 2001

CHEESE WHIZ

"I have said that the sanction regime is like Swiss cheese—that meant that they weren't very effective."

—*Washington, D.C., February 22, 2001*

"Brie and cheese."

—*What he imagines reporters eat, Crawford, Texas, August 23, 2001*

ATTACK OF THE SENATORS

"It would be a mistake for the United States Senate to allow any kind of human cloning to come out of that chamber."

—Washington, D.C., April 10, 2002

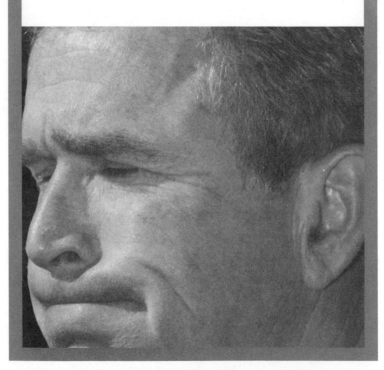

AIDES

"We're concerned about AIDS inside our
White House—make no mistake about it."

—*Washington, D.C., February 7, 2001*

SHOOT

"For every fatal shooting, there were
roughly three nonfatal shootings.
And, folks, this is unacceptable in
America. It's just unacceptable.
And we're going to do something
about it."

—*Philadelphia, Pennsylvania, May 14, 2001*

ALOFT

"Governor, thank you very much.
I am here to make an announcement that
this Thursday, ticket counters and airplanes
will fly out of Ronald Reagan Airport."

—*Arlington, Virginia, October 2, 2001*

TREED

"Arbolist . . . Look up the word.
I don't know, maybe I made it up.
Anyway, it's an arbo-tree-ist,
somebody who knows about trees."

Crawford, Texas, as quoted in USA Today,
August 21, 2001

NO BETTER

"I want to thank the dozens of welfare-to-
work stories, the actual examples of people
who made the firm and solemn commitment
to work hard to embetter themselves."

—*Washington, D.C., April 18, 2002*

OPTIMISTIC

"I believe the results of focusing our attention and energy on teaching children to read and having an education system that's responsive to the child and to the parents, as opposed to mired in a system that refuses to change, will make America what we want it to be—a literate country and a hopefuller country."

—*Washington, D.C., January 11, 2001*

BUT I WON'T

"You teach a child to read, and he or her will be able to pass a literacy test."

—*Townsend, Tennessee, February 21, 2001*

STATE MEANT

"Of all states that understands local control of schools, Iowa is such a state."

—*Council Bluffs, Iowa, February 28, 2001*

RESULTS

"It is time to set aside the old partisan
bickering and finger-pointing and name-
calling that comes from freeing parents to
make different choices for their children."

—Remarks on "parental empowerment in education,"
Washington, D.C., April 12, 2001

MISCONCEPTION

"We must have the attitude that every child
in America—regardless of where they're
raised or how they're born—can learn."

—New Britain, Connecticut, April 18, 2001

BILINGUALISM

"A lot of times in the rhetoric, people forget the facts. And the facts are that thousands of small businesses—Hispanically owned or otherwise—pay taxes at the highest marginal rate."

—*To the Hispanic Chamber of Commerce, Washington, D.C., March 19, 2001*

CALLING JUSTICE REHNQUIST

"I think the private savings accounts
ought to come from the payroll taxes
people contribute into the Social
Security trust. And this is an important
issue that I'm going to prioritize right
after I'm elected."

—Announcing a cabinet appointment,
December 20, 2000

EQUAL OPPORTUNITY

"The Senate needs to leave enough
money in the proposed budget to not only
reduce all marginal rates, but to eliminate
the death tax, so that people who build up
assets are able to transfer them from one
generation to the next, regardless of a
person's race."

—Washington, D.C., April 5, 2001

DEATH PENALTY I

"Those of us who spent time in the agricultural sector and in the heartland, we understand how unfair the death penalty is."

—*On the estate tax, Omaha, Nebraska, February 28, 2001*

"I talked about making the death tax permanent so that Rolf can pass his assets from—to a family member if he so chooses."

—*After meeting with small business owners, O'Fallon, Missouri, March 18, 2002*

DEATH PENALTY II

"I am mindful of the difference between the executive branch and the legislative branch. I assured all four of these leaders that I know the difference, and that difference is they pass the laws and I execute them."

—Washington, D.C., December 18, 2000

HANG IT

"I want to thank you for taking time out of your day to come and witness my hanging."

—At the dedication of his portrait, Austin, Texas, January 4, 2002

THE SOCIAL TEXTILE

"We'll be a country where the fabrics are made up of groups and loving centers."

—Western Michigan University,
Kalamazoo, Michigan, March 27, 2001

A BRIDGE TOO FAR

"I appreciate that question because
I, in the state of Texas, had heard a lot of
discussion about a faith-based initiative
eroding the important bridge between
church and state."

*—Question-and-answer session with the press,
January 29, 2001*

LIFE

"My pro-life position is I believe there's life. It's not necessarily based in religion. I think there's a life there, therefore the notion of life, liberty, and pursuit of happiness."

—*Quoted in the* San Francisco Chronicle, *January 23, 2001*

AMERICAN WAY I

"I can't tell you what it's like to be in Europe, for example, to be talking about the greatness of America. But the true greatness of America are the people."

—*Visiting the Jefferson Memorial,*
Washington, D.C., July 2, 2001

AMERICAN WAY II

"The great thing about America is everybody should vote."

—*Austin, Texas, December 8, 2000*

DICTATION

"If this were a dictatorship, it would be a heck of a lot easier, just so long as I'm the dictator."

—*Washington, D.C., December 18, 2000*

RESOLUTION

"This administration is doing everything we can to end the stalemate in an efficient way. We're making the right decisions to bring the solution to an end."

—*Washington, D.C., April 10, 2001*

DEALING

"And, yes, we're always interested in dealing with people who have harmed American citizens."

—Washington, D.C., February 25, 2002

MESSAGE

"Ann and I will carry out this
equivocal message to the world:
Markets must be open."

*—Swearing-in ceremony for Secretary of Agriculture Ann
Veneman, Washington, D.C., March 2, 2001*

GRACIAS

"Anyway, I'm so thankful and so
gracious—I'm gracious that my brother
Jeb is concerned about the hemisphere
as well."

—Miami, Florida, June 4, 2001

IMPORTUNITY

"The public education system in America is one of the most important foundations of our democracy. After all, it is where children from all over America learn to be responsible citizens, and learn to have the skills necessary to take advantage of our fantastic opportunistic society."

—*Santa Clara, California, May 1, 2002*

ABACK

"And we need a full affront on an energy crisis that is real in California and looms for other parts of our country if we don't move quickly."

—*Washington, D.C., March 29, 2001*

YES AND NO

"I'm sure you can imagine it's an unimaginable honor to live here."

—*In a White House address to agriculture leaders, June 18, 2001*

INCREDULOUS

"I'm also honored to be here with
the Speaker of the House—just happens
to be from the state of Illinois. I'd like to
describe the Speaker as a trustworthy man.
He's the kind of fellow who says when he
gives you his word he means it.
Sometimes that doesn't happen all the
time in the political process."

—*Chicago, Illinois, March 6, 2001*

ZONING

"It's about past seven in the evening here so we're actually in different time lines."

—Congratulating newly elected Philippine president Gloria Macapagal Arroyo, Washington, D.C., January 2001

GOING LONG

"And so, in my State of the—my State of the Union—or state—my speech to the nation, whatever you want to call it, speech to the nation—I asked Americans to give 4,000 years—4,000 hours over the next—the rest of your life—of service to America. That's what I asked—4,000 hours."

—Bridgeport, Connecticut, April 9, 2002

LOST HORIZON

"If there are warning signs on the horizon, we need to pay attention to them."

—Washington, D.C., December 21, 2000

"There's no question that the minute I got elected, the storm clouds on the horizon were getting nearly directly overhead."

—Washington, D.C., May 11, 2001

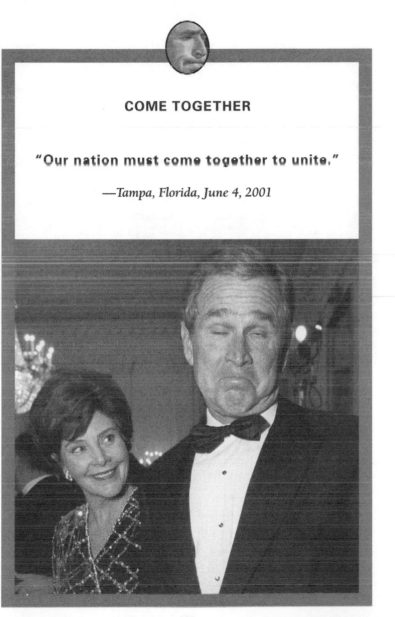

COME TOGETHER

"Our nation must come together to unite."

—*Tampa, Florida, June 4, 2001*

FRIENDSHIP

"I've got a preference for friends."

—After meeting with Prime Minister Jean Chrétien of Canada, Washington, D.C., February 5, 2001

"I confirmed to the prime minister that America appreciates our friendship."

—Ibid

JOBS, JOBS, JOBS

"But if you've been laid off of work, you're 100 percent unemployed, and I worry about it."

—Green Bay, Wisconsin, September 3, 2001

NO ACCOUNTING

"There was no malfeance involved. This was an honest disagreement about accounting procedures.... There was no malfeance, no attempt to hide anything."

—*White House press conference, Washington, D.C., July 8, 2002*

THE INVISIBLE HAND

"I understand how tender the free enterprise system can be."

—*White House press conference, Washington, D.C., July 9, 2002*

BUY AND HOLD

"And so, I hope investors, you know—
secondly, I hope investors hold investments
for periods of time—that I've always found
the best investments are those that you salt
away based on economics."

—Austin, Texas, January 4, 2001

CAP OFF

"The budget caps were busted, mightily so.
And we are reviewing with people like
Judd Gregg from New Hampshire and
others some budgetary reform measures
that will reinstate—you know, possibly
reinstate budgetary discipline. But the caps
no longer—the caps, I guess they're there.
But they didn't mean much."

—*Washington, D.C., February 5, 2001*

CALLING DR. FREUD

"My pan plays down an unprecedented
amount of our national debt."

—*Budget address to Congress, February 27, 2001*

PARK

"It's good to see so many friends here
in the Rose Garden. This is our first event
in this beautiful spot, and it's appropriate
we talk about policy that will affect people's
lives in a positive way in such a beautiful,
beautiful part of our national—really, our
national park system, my guess is you
would want to call it."

—*Washington, D.C., February 8, 2001*

FROZEN WASTE I

"There are some monuments where the
land is so widespread, they just encompass
as much as possible. And the integral part
of the—the precious part, so to speak
—I guess all land is precious, but the part
that the people uniformly would not want
to spoil, will not be despoiled. But there
are parts of the monument lands where
we can explore without affecting the
overall environment."

—Media round table, Washington, D.C.,
March 13, 2001

FROZEN WASTE II

"It would be helpful if we opened up
ANWR [Arctic National Wildlife Refuge].
I think it's a mistake not to. And I would
urge you all to travel up there and take
a look at it, and you can make the
determination as to how beautiful
that country is."

—*Press conference, Washington, D.C.,*
March 29, 2001

CONSERVATION

"Over the long term, the most effective way to conserve energy is by using energy more efficiently."

—*Radio address, May 12, 2001*

GAS

"Natural gas is hemispheric. I like to call it hemispheric in nature because it is a product that we can find in our neighborhoods."

—*Austin, Texas, December 20, 2000*

CALLING BUFFY

"One of the interesting initiatives we've taken in Washington, D.C., is we've got these vampire-busting devices. A vampire is a—a cell deal you can plug in the wall to charge your cell phone."

—*Denver, Colorado, August 14, 2001*

ENERGY POWER

"The California crunch really is the result of not enough power-generating plants and then not enough power to power the power of generating plants."

—*Interview with* The New York Times, *January 14, 2001*

"We've also got to understand, in order to power the power-generating plants that are now being built in California, we need more energy."

—*Washington, D.C., April 24, 2001*

WITH CHILD

"The way I like to put it is this.
There's no bigger issue for the president
to remind the moms and dads of America,
if you happen to have a child, be
fortunate to have a child."

—To Treasury Department employees,
March 7, 2001

JENNA

"Maybe she'll be able to join us in Florida.
If not, she can clean out her room."

—On his daughter's recovery from an appendectomy,
December 26, 2000

DEEP

"The reason I believe in a large tax cut because it's what I believe."

—Washington, D.C., December 18, 2000

DEEPER

"Home is important. It's important to have a home."

—Crawford, Texas, February 18, 2001

DEEPEST

"There's nothing more deep than recognizing Israel's right to exist. That's the most deep thought of all. . . . I can't think of anything more deep than that right."

—*Washington, D.C., March 13, 2002*

LEGACIES

"There's no such thing as legacies. At least, there is a legacy, but I'll never see it."

—*To Catholic leaders at the White House, January 31, 2001*

GIVEN

"I admit it, I am not one of the great linguists."

—To Tom Brokaw, Inside the Real West Wing, *January 23, 2001*

ONE FOR TWO

**"I've coined new words, like,
'misunderstanding' and 'Hispanically.'"**

*—Radio-Television Correspondents Association dinner,
Washington, D.C., March 29, 2001*

HISPANICALLY SPEAKING

**"Over 75 percent of white Americans own
their home, and less than 50 percent of
Hispanos and African Americans don't own
their home. And that's a gap, that's a
homeownership gap. And we've got to do
something about it."**

—Cleveland, Ohio, July 1, 2002

AND REMEMBER

"The thing that's important for me is
to remember what's the most
important thing."

—*Moline Elementary School near Moline Acres,
St. Louis, Missouri, February 20, 2001*

Photo Credits

Win McNamee/Reuters/Timepix—8, 24, 34, 57, 87

AFP/CORBIS—12, 15, 20, 27, 39, 44, 46, 50, 59, 69, 73

Bob Daemrrich/Corbis Sygma—10, 58

Brooks Kraft/Corbis Sygma—13, 66

Kevin Lamarque/Reuters/Timepix—32

Joseph Sohm; ChromoSohm Inc./CORBIS—29, 72, 74

AP Photo/Joe Marquette—16, 62

AP Photo/John Gaps III—49, 83

AP Photo/Eric Gay—41

AP Photo/Eric Draper—22, 53

Reuters Newmedia Inc./CORBIS—21, 28, 42, 52, 64, 71, 80, 85